Light at the Seam

POEMS

Light at the Seam

Joseph Bathanti

Louisiana State University Press

Baton Rouge

Published by Louisiana State University Press

lsupress.org

LSU Press Paperback Original

DESIGNER: Mandy McDonald Scallan

TYPEFACE: Arno Pro

Cover photo: *Lost on the Road to Oblivion,* by Carl Galie.

Cataloging-in-Publication Data are available from the Library of Congress.

ISBN 978-0-8071-7692-4 (pbk.: alk. paper) — ISBN 978-0-8071-7732-7 (pdf) — ISBN 978-0-8071-7741-9 (epub)

For Joan, Jacob & Beckett

Mater Gloriosa

Praise the summer mourning cloaks,
blue-rimmed, massed across the valley.

Praise the cumulonimbus,
the daughters of song.

Praise the catbird thieving suet,
swaying like the cantor at high Requiem.

Praise the small white butterflies from childhood,
paten-wings, shawls of ether.

Praise the world of names—
Tuckasegee, Oconaluftee, Wayah.

—IN LOVING MEMORY: Kathryn Stripling Byer

Contents

Acknowledgments

Grateful acknowledgment is extended to the editors of the following journals, in which some of these poems, in some cases different versions and with different titles, first appeared: *Anglican Theological Review:* "Floyd County, Kentucky"; *Appalachian Heritage:* "Glade Creek Falls" and "Day Lily"; *Appalachian Journal:* "Cleaving to That," "Kayford," "Flyrock," "Dulcimer," "Headwaters of the New," and "Sundial, West Virginia"; *Appalachian Lit:* "Agnus Dei"; *Appalachian Magazine:* "Rainey's Trailer"; *Asheville Poetry Review:* "A Map from Clyde Hollifield"; *Beloit Poetry Journal:* "Postdiluvian: Mingo County, West Virginia"; *Chautauqua: The Literary Journal of Chautauqua Institution:* "The Vale"; *Christian Century:* "Blessed Thistle"; *Fourth River:* "April Snow" and "Behold"; *Greensboro Review:* "The Assumption"; *Hollins Critic:* "From This Fair Green House" and "Fall Webworms"; *Iodine Poetry Review:* "The Face of the River"; *Kestrel:* "Oracle"; *New Letters:* "Runoff"; Orion Blog of *Orion Magazine:* "Limbo"; *Platte Valley Review:* "First Linville Creek"; *Potato Eyes:* "The Mole"; *Raleigh Review:* "Light at the Seam" and "The Windows of Heaven"; *Red Dirt Forum:* "Mater Gloriosa"; *Shining Rock Poetry Anthology & Review:* "Agnus Dei"; *Southern Cultures:* "The Coal Miner's Wife"; *Spiritus: A Journal of Christian Spirituality:* "Removing the Mountain from the Coal"; and *St. Andrews Review:* "My Mother and Father."

Thanks also to the editors of the anthologies in which the following poems, in some cases different versions and with different titles, first appeared: *MOTIF* 2

Chance: Come What May: "Evensong"; *Reflections on the New River: New Essays, Poems and Personal Stories:* "Near Fayette Station"; and *Step around the Mountain: Southern Appalachian Mountains:* "Sentences."

I must also extend to my friend, the award-winning photographer Carl Galie, profound gratitude and great affection. Eighteen of the poems in this collection were inspired by Carl's photographic exhibition *Lost on the Road to Oblivion: The Vanishing Beauty of Coal Country,* a project that he embarked on in order to reclaim his sense of home and the truth embodied in that yearning. His work takes the viewer on a journey through the Southern Appalachians while documenting the practice of mountaintop removal, as well as its collateral fallout, in a series of haunting, exquisite images of an endangered natural environment. The story of our friendship and collaboration defies summary; suffice to say, however, that it turned on a series of uncanny—mystical, by my lights—convergences. Once I saw Carl's breathtaking photographs, I seemed to have no choice but to write about them. Without him, this book would not be possible. He handed me another world.

I

The Assumption

Now at the fall of night, you shocks,

Still bend your heads like kind and humble kings

The way you did this golden morning when you saw God's

Mother passing,

While all our windows fill and sweeten

With the mild vespers of the hay and barley.

—THOMAS MERTON

From "The Evening of the Visitation"

Removing the Mountain from the Coal

Lorries, at that altitude,
defy gravity, cross-hatching
a bric-a-brac of switchback Zs—

their unearthed ruin in the clouds,
its overburden in the valley.
Something with not only the will,

but the ordnance (ammonium
nitrate) to blow 400 meters
off the mountain's frontal lobe of cortex

where memory once construed:
its infinite vaults and archives—
the oldest extant range on earth—

a record of the moment
on the third day of Genesis—
when Jehovah whispered,

Let the dry land appear,
then the transcripts of what followed
ever after. Gone. Gray matter

and emerald striae tier. Black
twinkle vast impoundments.
Slurries lurk. Across the horizon—

eastern Kentucky, Tennessee,
all of West Virginia, into western
Virginia—summits picket:

massive reds, yellow autumnal fire.
Light breaks about their faces.
Understories flower.

Floyd County, Kentucky

No lintel to speak of,
but a chicken wire screen
door hinged on twelve-inch

block and lattice, jittering,
wind chimes knelling,
each time a charge grunts—

off-thunder rumbling the hollows.
The masonry had been sound;
shock split the seams: gashes

of mortar where it's been repointed,
caulked sashes.
Number 2 pine gone ashy, fixing

to rot; the dooryard
held in a brazen of peonies,
rickety picket once-white

to corset them, pink-red
like the font in *Luke*
where Jesus says to John:

. . . the Son of Man hath not where to lay His head.
Just inside hangs a woman's shawl,
slick, see-through as onion skin;

maybe it's parchment,
scrivened in bodement,
the letters gone to blood.

It can drive you to your knees:
how folks set out flowers,
and look upon the earth.

Glade Creek Falls

In a canyon of the gorge
pours Glade Creek Falls—
homage, as is proper, to the New.

Only the Nile is older.
Obscenely young, prey to impulse,
we indenture to the glade—

our trysting place—and to each other.
Like the Bible, like mythography,
we truss, foretold, in writ scrolls of eternity.

True love among children
is psilocybin; what we eat wild
from this earth claims us.

Outcroppings lounge in cloud mantles.
The water attempts modesty,
but may not veil itself.

It sprays from its secret cave,
evanescent, quicksilver. Twisted
hemlocks screw into bedrock.

Poplars loose leaves over deep green pools.
The sun is barred, but for shadow, mottled.
On a fainting couch of rock

we strike our troth. Yet
whelped as I am in the quaking red
syllables of Gospel, Fayette County,

I know sin black as bituminous.
Just so, I remain my Savior's primal witness.
Named and fabled, the world hatches.

Daylily

Each year, the centurial black walnut
threatens to expire,

yet flowers branch by branch, bud by bud,
magisterial in its hour.

Sunlit moss berms Linville Creek.
Yellow rock tablets lull the stream.

Upon the aged plank bridge,
in velvet sprawls a mink.

You, lily, feathery, fluted,
pistil and stamen, bathe

there at the bank, like Artemis,
for just a day, gazing

at the clouds hovering the ridge
beyond which dreams the next life

vaulted in the firmament.
You burst into this world through desire,

that alone your imprimatur.
Yet make no mistake:

you are permitted entry through grace.
You may not beg for this pittance,

however ephemeral, burning as you are.
It befalls you. I should stop now.

A daylily does not want for a man,
but sainthood, ablaze

for a lone revolution on earth's axis,
then offering itself in sacrifice,

kin to those brazen red-headed martyrs—
trussed pendent to your stem,

puckered, collapsed parasol,
loved but once in flaming thrall.

Fall Webworms

They arrive this year a month early, July,
another augur of weather awry,
and spin silk tents

in the black locust's upper stories.
Larger daily purl the webs,
gauzy at dawn; come noon,

high sun, gossamer;
spectral by the sturgeon moon,
across which kite thunderheads

crashed on Agnes Ridge, lashed
with hail at its frost line.
Within each gauntlet depended from a branch

hunch veiled widows in white bridals,
cradling their stillborn.
They tell the jilted future of this plat.

From riven bark,
locust thorns thrive in poison pairs.
These apparitions are but nesting

caterpillars, latched to natal trees,
one day to emerge as moths, winter white,
the winged ample sleeves of nyads.

Yet, in their instars,
they defoliate whole forests.
Lightning gattles the tin

above the baby's head.
The sky misremembers.
Nightmare trembles in its bed.

The Assumption

Relentless as the season itself,
the gleaning, the thresh,

the yellow Vermeer baler
grinds in the wake

of the lethal haymow, scything
the dogleg on the Watauga shank

of East Tennessee—
clef of ink on the plat.

On a particular August evening,
in sacrificial silence,

the first leaf floats from Billings' maple.
The first buckeye rends nocturnal

solitude off the black road crown.
Woolly worms take their interminable walk

into winter-clad robes of sooth.
Webworms sleeve the locust in smoke.

In praise of stigmata,
dogwood berries bleed.

The next day, a Friday, the 15th,
the Feast of the Assumption—

the taking up of the Blessed Mother,
body and soul, into Heaven—

the families who lease the doctor's land hay.
Come the gloaming valley

tractors and chuffing balers swoon
aslant the windrows—well after nightfall,

baling in the bore of a dozen pickup headlamps.
Outlandish bundles: long grass green;

infant asters, fetal blue; Queen Anne's lace,
its impersonator, wild carrot;

gentians; pricked orange purses
of daylilies; and colonies,

whole kingdoms, of snake, vole, dragonfly,
rabbit, whirring ethnographies of insects

—trussed in moonlit whorls
of cylindrical blond brushstroke.

Crows chant high in white sycamores.
The bales gather vibrato.

Blue mantles of chaff
in the mist off Linville Creek,

the glorious apparition of fireflies
in Our Lady's tiara, as she rises—

tresses of sorrow, tresses
of praise, from the harvest.

My Mother and Father

Eight stout bales of coiled hay
since first threshing, May—

three, maybe four, years ago—
lay at the edge of the swales,

somehow forgotten by the folks
who lease Billings' dogleg,

and tend tobacco that glows,
of harvest, as if the sun bled

the plow soles. This morning
the monarch bides the lavender thistle-

down, wings opening, closing,
marking time in its imaginal phase,

dispersing eggs among the last autumn flowers.
On the creek bank, deer grind

green husks, hulls like shark skin,
the ancient chestnut drops.

Their cuneiform prints fork the silt
left from August flash floods.

The fog is shot with blue-gray beams,
gauzy portal to everlasting.

Strangers walk here,
with their burdens and assignations.

They read the writing spiders' ideograms,
legible at first light, rimed in dew—

in seconds, deliquesced.
Webs cup the rose of Sharon.

Those two lone cedars in the gap—
my mother and father.

Blessed Thistle

July, it sidles from the spermy loam,
lost for a spate among the dripping tares—
wild flowers scroll strangled in dross and roam—
sprouting bristly heads of purple hairs

clear to the warped planks spanning Linville Creek.
Choirs of milk thistle congregate the swale,
burst from Vilas to raise a church: . . . *the meek* . . .
shall inherit the earth. Upon this vale

such flowers shrive, and prick eternity:
spines of spiked cane, inedible, austere.
Come haying, it takes vows of poverty,
chastity, and obedience. White hair

flares from its wimple. Fireflies torch the night—
the thousand thousand thuribles of light.

II

The Windows of Heaven

The sides of the hollow, as we got further in, more naked and scalped, more trees coming down, and up above, mostly just scraggly weeds, the ground deep-ribbed with erosion, and I told myself, yes, this is where the floods come from. From the busted ponds and the confused new shape of the land. From how the land has forgot where the water should go, so the water is just running off every which way.

—ANN PANCAKE

From *Strange as This Weather Has Been*

Postdiluvian: Mingo County, West Virginia

The day dawns repentant,
sky blue. Union Mission

hauls in food and blankets, toys.
Pigeon Creek, now slaked,

plumb in its banks, yet still flexing
at its gouged shoulders, is sick

green-brown in slabs of sunlight—
dull as a gorged serpent.

It's had too much to drown—
more mine-rain runoff

than Mingo tribal land would suffer.
Its breach was obscene—

massing diluvia bent on blood feud.
Sycamores snapped in tandem.

Roil stormed the house,
cleaved its seams and sockets,

white shakes skived in coils from its face—
the Pigeon in the children's room,

counterpanes of water
draping spinet and chifferobe.

The roof caved the porch.
The saltbox jackknifed,

joists gone for tinder. A good house—
built righteously with gravity

and optimism, signed verily
in sacrifice and prophecy—

it swamped, then sundered, vitals bared,
the yard washed off to Pike County

through the Tug River Valley.
The bones of the Hatfields and McCoys

bristle in beds of coal silt.
Nary a crow circles.

From This Fair Green House

From this house,
fair green, trimmed white—
Hale Fork Road off Route
850, Floyd County, Kentucky—
someone turned away,
in good faith, rest assured,
tithed it and its acres to coal
and whatever promises
forth-came from barter.
Now in winter, ridges stripped,
naked elms in rags of snow—
not a single bird to keep them decent,
the sky a disappearing blue.
The house perches on pylons.
Water shaped its plat:
Left Fork Little Creek Levisa
Fork, to the north Pitts Fork.
Gone are the porch stairs,
no door, panes punched out.
The threshold lies there—
not breathing. Thatched in tin,
the gable window gapes
one-eyed, moony. Tattooed
in the gray tallow roadbed:
ditches, blasted culverts, the deep
tread of haul trucks. A slip
of grass skirts a fallow field.
From above, stray cries
twist the hollows—
vestige terrain forbidden,
crossed over in echo.

Headwaters of the New

(for Pat Beaver)

Someone who believes

                                     in a single drop of water

                must guide you.

No map of this bramble

                                                steep, its storied green:

                mossy black rock,

                        pink angiosperm,

                lichen, leather-leaf,

                                  stonewort, ferns,

                                      compost of millennia

             suckling the very tree—

                    anonymous as Mary,

                            burning for the sun

             through its canopy

                    of forebears—that parts

                                its roots to cradle

          the source. Genuflect.

Tell no one.

                                Down Snake Mountain

                                  licks the New.

The Windows of Heaven

. . . in the second month, the seventeenth day of the month, the same day were all the
fountains of the great deep broken up, and the windows of heaven were opened.
   — GENESIS 6:11

Down Coal River Mountain,
where gorges slurry atop Eagle seam,

water leaks from invisible understories:
one drop, then one drop more until

revealing itself, quickened,
in the gap malformed, flashing

on its back the chromium
light that augurs flood,

departing its branch, swaggering
the hairpin, jewel weed

slickened to its banks, yellow
buds drowned, flickering

the whiptail. Phoebes chant.
Crows set up black on wires.

Spotted cows slosh muck to the knoll.
Then it's hurtling drunk the swale,

airborne, creek no more,
but cock-strong river, gouting spit,

wronged in some Shakespearean mien:
sizzling rain, simmered in the troposphere—

three, four inches, too little time,
too sparse a vessel—gravity

smearing it through the valley.
Upon the land gathers a biblical

quietus before it explodes
the culvert at the hollow crosshairs

where roads conflux and houses,
that once believed they'd be a town,

cower at the surge.
The wind spells its knots.

The sky throbs.
Folks huddle on the rise

beyond Rainey's swamped trailer
and watch it come on.

Runoff

Vast white sheets of hay bale wrap
sail through the flume—

like the mine has stripped its beds
and flung the linen, sluiced

through a blown shaft—stupendous
as clouds in the black spindrift—

to the runoff. Up Agnes Ridge,
panicked angus slue the flooded swale.

Purple virgin's bower, twined
to rusted barbed wire, rends

in the spume. The sun,
93 million miles off,

yet kin to water, created the same day,
appears behind the curtain of rain—

everything at once antithetical.
We pretend with the children

that making for higher ground is a game.
Born to elevation, gravity tugs them.

Lording above brims the slurry pond,
quaking with raindrops.

The Horton girl—not but three—
like reading from a ledger

names the swept-up:
Miss Shipley's iris,

Isaac's whiffletree,
Pollyanne's mule cart,

Jordan's Caddy hubcaps,
that vain vexed rooster of Galloway.

The hoard defies tallying:
goods wrested from folks who bled for them.

The valley's oldest farm is underwater,
the house to its blue gable wings.

Fate Biddix's cabbage field flashes by,
heads bobbing—a tale of epic slaughter.

We cover the children's eyes,
and scurry for the knoll.

Rainey's Trailer

Swoony, tattered tin shakes,
red-gone-rust, splayed siding

shuddering in the wind,
on a warped scrap-wood

frame drilled with carpenter
ants—stripped, scavenged

to soured batting
and black-funk ply-board—

in cinquefoil and Saint-John's-wort,
along Linville Creek.

Bedclothes, gown and bonnet,
a girl-child's play-pretties,

scrap and curio:
gone to char in what's left

of the mud dooryard—
rope swing snared in the white pine,

rusted axe-head scored in its trunk;
frozen hemlock shivered

into punk wood; a well bit.
Swarmed in lavender whisks,

a butterfly bush engulfs the trailer—
a fable's hexed weir—

sown in thrift and profligacy,
a life moored to a single patch of earth

fetched by a woman no one remembers—
who spirited off in the nocturnes

with her baby daughter. Of summer,
within its gutted rectangle,

mourning cloaks, in requiem, hover
with tiger swallowtails—

fanning black and gold bellows,
ascending through the pierced roof.

April Snow

The grass whelps in biblical mien—
mowers spend themselves—

a writ of greenest green,
spangled in sunbursts,

as if Van Gogh decided on
the remnant petrified thistle,

the first violets at his feet,
and painted Billings' meadow.

Robins pompously swagger.
Swifts (little crosses)

jet above them. Birdsong.
Frog-song. Early spring

by habit exaggerates itself,
the green a blinding recognition.

To the ridge mount pines and firs.
Ancient hardwoods swell

by the day with bringing forth.
Blackberry whip the swales,

its cane shrove-purple
from the long winter.

In Sugar Grove, daffodils worship
on the abandoned Ruritan diamond.

Bases bleach in the dirt.
Home plate is a pentagon.

It forgets nothing.
Life is more than fable,

but never stops stunning earth.
And so: hushed clouds, sheepish,

sheep-shaped, yet foretold,
slip over Snake Den Mountain.

Their shadows blanket the valley floor.
The snow they release is inevitable.

This is how we must think of it—
inevitable—how we must welcome it,

the white behest of silence,
the green beneath it jade, milky.

Agnus Dei

The shearer's come horseback from Solo—
shaven head, golden beard,
ear hoops.

The ewe cowers in the crib corner.
When she tries to run,
he clamps her between his chaps,

muscles her to her rump.
She sits the straw floor,
prim as a sheep at tea, beneath thatch,

in a picture book,
fore-hooves limp at the fetlock.
Her eyes are indigo,

black-slash irises,
murky augur of cataracts,
teeth like feed corn.

Perhaps her name is Esther, Millicent:
high-born, elegant,
about to remark in Shetland lilt

on the unseasonable chill,
incessant mizzle—jolly enough,
kettle on the hob, snug

in her ancient gnarl of Appalachia.
Yet pensive, resigned to this final shearing,
she's exceeded her life span by half,

her carded dower the woolens
of each baby born heir to this plat.
Clippers rev, then flash the comb

and blade shears, sweat of the shearer—
black leather singlet,
scarlet bandana,

flannel trousers—as he carves her,
cleaved to him, from her weir.
His work is a mercy.

She closes her eyes,
rocks back in forgettery.
Fleece scrolls from her—

bound volumes, therein archived:
the milk-tooth of a bear cub,
an eaglet's feather,

a bard owl's ossified heart,
wedding band, possum skull,
Cherokee potsherds,

the 31st chapter of Deuteronomy
torn from King James.
Released, burnished, and blinding

as a chalice—Immaculata—
she barges into Holy Saturday's dripping
emerald, bundled in fog, pink

the mayapple blossoms,
then runs for the moon dangling
from its nail on Agnes Ridge.

Beyond the Shipley line,
from the balcony ornamenting
the front gable wings

of the Horton place,
strains a mandolin, then a woman
singing: *hard-hearted Barbry Allen.*

To its shoulders in flood dread,
Linville Creek readies its bed.
Shrouded mountains genuflect.

Limbo

From the Latin word *limbus,* "fringe" or "edge," Limbo is

considered to be "outside of Heaven."

—*The Catholic Encyclopedia*

Limbo

In *Almost Heaven,*
Carl Galie's photograph—
composed from the vantage
of Heaven—I finally witness
Limbo, precisely as I pictured it:
an endless sweep of the ancient
Appalachian chain, just the peaks,
in autumnal brilliance,
to their chins in cottony vapor,
an imprimatur of fathomless white
from here to Nineveh.
Limbo is indeed *almost Heaven*—
but decidedly not Heaven—
where unbaptized babies,
ever-smoldering
with original sin, are sentenced,
for eternity, never to gaze
upon the brow of Yahweh—
though the *Catechism* confirms
they're not in pain,
happy at this altitude
among the infinite
pixels of the firmament
swaddling them, excluded,
in clouds—the afterlife,
created on the second day.

Kayford

(for Larry Gibson)

On the spine
of Kayford Mountain,
secreted among
aged trees, a moment
from surrendering
their raiment
to the long stark
of winter, the last
rampart of homes
braces at the edge
of the mine,
looming above
what it once shelved on—
the highest crown,
now erased—
a quarter century
ago: decomposed
vaults, exposed
vein walls, spooled
declivities,
craters of gray,
altitude devoured
by draglines,
then trundled off
in leviathan
haul trucks over
blasted roads.
No Trespassing
impends
a large red
caution.

Cleaving to That

Headstones, old
as the New, shudder
and stray, ever-weighted
down among the few
blue bouquets, faded
in the wake of drag lines,
haul trucks.
Often they topple
when the charge
lays up under them.
Across their faces,
numbers and letters witness
the summit's dwindled census.
Men and women,
even infants—angel stones,
tatted granite on the green
grave floor—claw
at purchase, give out
cleaving to that
clattered bald yonder.

Flyrock

The pre-blast siren sounds
5 minutes prior
to the fired charge—a trinity

of 5-second shrieks
5 seconds apart,
then quakes the peak,

splits the core,
mountains of war. Loosed
upon detonation,

collateral flyrock
from the blast zone,
60 meters off

at the mine removal site—
the span of a church nave—strikes
the Stanley Family Cemetery

on Kayford Mountain—
seven generations, tombs
to the 1700s.

Black shale pocks the earth,
like bullets, strafes the very names
hewn in ledger stone—

ancestors of this altitude
exploded from their dreams.
Down below wend slurry streams.

Near Fayette Station

Well north of East Mountain—
after Glen Jean,

the last town conjuring a woman,
until Jane Lew, even further north,

beyond the 88-story bridge
levitating above the New River Gorge—

you pass in Oak Hill
the Church of Saints Peter and Paul.

Make the Sign of the Cross,
then again

at the West Virginia Office of Mines.
Genuflect to Leonard of Noblac,

patron saint of coal miners,
his charge and chisel, his martyrdom

in the seam of black Sun Mine.
Beneath Route 19,

Wolf Creek unravels
through its boulder flume,

near Fayette Station,
speed-blurred, white

as the cumulonimbi
coursing the gap, into the open

where the Wolf rants into the New,
heaving in its chasm.

Oracle

(for Carl Galie)

Chestnut Ridge lords above its colliers
secreted in seams of Royal Mine.

Smoke plumes from the company's plant stacks.
Patch-town kids bide clouds of coal.

What must they spy in the boiling brume?
The sky's caught fire.

Still they play the game:
a herd of buffalo,

a monkey, ram, an ape,
a shambling wyvern,

the Four Horsemen of the Apocalypse—
a tribunal of freaks. Scary enough—

the power to imagine anything:
Shroud of Turin; fetal angels,

eyes yet to open, robed
in sable carbon; miners

swinging thuribles, foaming incense,
from Purgatory; Saint John

the Evangelist coughing in the shaft house;
a '50s noir of Armageddon.

Such clouds: Lie down in them.
Stir them like an oracle:

see what poor people look like.
Things are taking shape.

Sentences

It is true that it is the men that goes in, but is us
that carries the mine inside.
—DIANE GILLIAM FISHER
"Explosion at Winco No. 9" (from *Kettle Bottom*)

(for Ernest Hill & Jimmie Bell)

The work of rescue
through Cumberland granite
favors piety,
the liturgy
of pump and drill,
dirge and hymn,
the feudal knell
of blade on stone
nine days without respite—
the tumult of hearts
dredging hope
overlong.

The women are statues,
mouths set in chiseled lines,
gaunt dresses;
the querulous, yearning
faces of their children,
baby birds,
whose portion
lay swaddled
in the ebon seam.

At the shaft house,
they queue
awaiting the cage—
finally: blue lips,
black fingers,
nine days bearded,
notes pinned to their blouses.

These were not men beholden
to words on a page:
the flailing sentences
their hands willed
toward farewell,
syllables tailing,
down and
gently down,
too faint
to make out.

Sundial, West Virginia

Children take sick from powdered coal,
loaded into freight cars from a silo

half a soccer field
from their Marsh Fork schoolyard,

then doused with bonding agents
to suppress the dust.

Twelve hundred feet above their cubbies
hovers an earthen dam—

behind it, bibbed, the gray impoundment:
2.8 billion gallons of coal sludge.

From the gouged peak, subdural,
lobotomized, serpentine switchbacks

weave a cat's cradle into the grade-rooms.
Snared in the hourglass—

instead of sand, slurry trickles—
kids convert feet into meters,

gauge the rate at which rain falls,
the agonizing pace of drizzle.

They study terminal velocity,
the likely speed of a downslope flash flood

loosed from a suddenly ruptured levee,
memorize the Periodic Table

of Chemical Elements, commit
to their vocabulary: *watershed, toxic,*

overburden, subsidiary, arsenic,
mercury, chromium, cadmium,

boron, nickel, selenium.
They pledge allegiance;

return thanks in the lunch hall;
at recess skip rope, play jacks,

Johnny on a Pony;
sing *Little Red Caboose.*

Their primer is gravity.
The first bell signals, barely

this side of glory. Sundial
casts its shadow on the hour.

(Marsh Fork Elementary opened its new school, a few miles down
Coal River Road, in Naoma, in January of 2013).

The Face of the River

*Very slowly, his expression changed as if he were gradually seeing appear
what he didn't know he'd been looking for.*
   —FLANNERY O'CONNOR
     "The River"

A little brown-haired boy,
four or five, alone,
under the Route 114 Bridge
in camo shorts tugged down
by the ballast of the New—
revealing a band of white,
hidden from the sun,
below his waist.
Baby fat puckers his wrists.

He's been warned of drowning,
that he shouldn't wade.
But he is two people—like us all—
and, so-minded, confident;
as yet, not obliged to fate;
nor does he fear water.

Standing in the circle, tiding out
concentrically from his entry,
he is epicenter of everything:
the river, trees scaling ranges
riven with coal,
kestrel, hawk, and sun—
all of Montgomery County,
West Virginia.

Like Narcissus, he bends to his likeness.
Forbidden to sound, immured
forever in the ancient New,
his twin ascends from his bed,
little hands reaching
for the face of the river.

For an instant, they're permitted union,
conjoined at the surface like acrobats:
the water boy balancing
on his fingertips
his earthly brother staring
through illusory vectors of light
into his own eyes reflected
on the sheer plane of the New.

Boar

He preys over the carcass of a doe,
left in the autumn windrows.
Once, climbing Agnes Ridge,
I'd come across him in the blackberry:
abiding, carnal—
matted, shaggy coat,
stupendous head.
He could have had me.
He let me know as much:
ancient face, haunted leer—
near smile.
There would be no mercy.
Today he seesaws on his haunches,
as he strips the doe:
his bestial gorge and groan,
tugging her up like taffy.
Finished, he rears and faces me—
safe, in midair, watching
from the balcony.
Cold columns of vapor writhe.
Solstice clouds,
from Johnson County, Tennessee,
storm Snake Den Mountain.
What's wrought in this valley's beyond our ken.
This creature—charged out of Shakespeare,
tusk-sharpened sneer,
gut-string pigtail, on his chest
a white pentagonal smear—
kin to werewolves.

Evensong

At opposite ends of the feeder,
dangling from the buckeye
by a sliver of jute,
a cardinal and indigo bunting
feed, seemingly oblivious
to the blue and scarlet other,
their self-absorption
an ongoing evolutionary tick
completed this very instant.

Birdseed falls into the tall grass
under the tree.
The cardinal flies off,
upsetting the feeder's ballast.
It sways, wildly
at first, then less
and then less until less,
like a hypnotist's gold watch,
while the bunting,
fading by degrees
into the falling blue spell
of evening remains
perfectly still.

IV

Light at the Seam

Prisms seize on any light, even the tallow
fat candle rendering its bacon smell hazily through
the night; girls wear flowers at their weddings,
and their gowns stay miraculously white.

—ANN E. MICHAEL

From "Miners"

The Vale

Depended from the brow above our cabin
keens the widow's shack, a tipsy slab
of creosote and poison ivy
her pigmy wethers grind without pause.
Davidson's sheep fatten on her grass.

The slope stinks of silage.
The widow's in this summer;
we've yet to spy her.
Her son's a preacher, Church of God.
He beats his wife, her voice shrill,

his effeminate once whipped to wrath.
The ragged robins eavesdrop.
The swales blue with them.
The gap absorbs each backhand,
chambered across the valley.

A tribe of deer—
buck, doe, their recent fawn,
spots seasoning its deliquescent vest—
feed off fallen chestnuts,
crunching the barbed hulls.

They twitch, gather their legs, and still.
The buck drops a spiked planet from his mouth,
and gazes into the darkening firmament.
The doe soughs alarm.
They cut to the brink and disappear.

Coyotes loop the ridge,
yowling like the Purgatory-forgotten.
Calves sob. Then gunfire. Echo
strobes the valley. At this altitude,
you cannot reckon by sound—

and no such thing as kilter.
The sheriff's Crown Victoria rips up
the wash and carts off the son.
Morning, he's back, on his moped.
The earth curves.

First Linville Creek

Dark the coldest
morning so far. Bright
stars, deserted road.
The first seconds of light
needle earth along
its crease. The cows
favor black—black
steeped in rectitude.
They'll not speak
against the escarpment,
the icy peak
spilling over it.
They are apart, shawls
of rime, resolute
as martyrs: the shriven days
left to them in this
fallow cabbage field.
The dawn moon hovers
the valley, precise,
monolithic—
like the exposed host.
Light now enough
to see the mammoth
crows strutting among
the cows. Not an apple
in the orchard,
the Coffindaffer
crosses at first
Linville Creek ablaze.

Behold

The storm shakes
blood from the hemlock,
then ceases
in paroxysms. Across
the shocked vale
shudders silence
in its wake. The sky
in a feat of grief
turns lavender
the gap. Behold:
the first haying's golden
bales sprawl against
the mountain sole—
so bereft the drenched
crows weep.

Dulcimer

(For Lisa Moore)

I bought it
on Friendship Church Road
in Aho for $50:

a four-string that rings
bright as the day it was strung
by Squire Elzie Weaver,

the luthier that built it.
The sound board's finish
is spruce pine, steamed

to hourglass-shape the sides.
The inner's oak for tone,
body black walnut,

ivory tuning pegs,
frets are bone.
In long hips below its waist

swirl slashed sound holes,
seahorse-shaped;
and, in the slender bodice above,

on either side of the sound bar,
bore 9 punctures,
like .22 slug eyelets,

auger-clean—
arranged in an S.
Sealed with hide or fish glue, one,

then Ruby shellac cut with alcohol;
chamfered edges sanded round,
smooth, though nothing dainty;

brown as turned earth,
the blood-heft of a newborn.
I studied it for initials,

some signature, fetish, or brand.
I pored over it with my tongue,
and found nary a trace of Elzie.

Pluck it with a quill,
slide and stop the strings
with a stick.

Use your fingers;
it takes, to praise,
a calloused hand.

A Map from Clyde Hollifield

Somewhere on the easternmost fringes of Buncombe County, Clyde Hollifield leads a
taciturn existence far from the madding crowd. But his reputation casts a long shadow.

  —ALLISON FRANK

    From "Outside the Lines"

A preacher owns the Fina station
at the Sugar Hill fork to Bat Cave.
In the hollow sunk behind it,
an old woman in a rough-cut plank
shack sells slab wood,
cigarettes and bait, white liquor.
The town is dry. She'll tell you
what roadhouses to stray from.
Keep to Catawba Avenue:
past Four Oaks Fish Camp,
Faw's and Old Fort School,
the women from the yarn mill
smoking at noon dinner on the curb.
Back off the access road,
against the first outlying conifers
of the distant Pisgah,
looms Two Trees' big white house,
its balcony and spooky scrollwork—
a temple against the tree line:
seekers the world over come
to McDowell County to be healed by him.
Turn left at the depot
onto the last of Main Street.
The railroad once traveled
here to Asheville,
through the Swannanoa Tunnel—
before there was law—
to Cherokee County.
Boxcars, scrivened with hobo glyphs,
hulk in the sidings.
Three stories high

on its pedestal of river rock—
like the Ten Commandments—
juts the gigantic granite arrowhead
(dedicated 1930)—
the symbol of peace,
after the slaughter,
between the pioneers and Indians.
A right on Mill Creek
and beyond Andrews Geyser
until the road narrows and ends
at a washed-out gravel two-track
where the headwaters
of the Catawba burble, then
the cloaked ascent to Black Mountain—
if you have the stomach for seven miles
of blind spindle switchbacks,
and a map from Clyde Hollifield.

The Mole

There is a poison,
yet I did nothing
but watch the earth tremble;
and, with a week's rain,
two small trees toppled
in the orchard
where finally I saw one
drowned in his own ditch,
an apple floating with him:
a child's long-lashed
astonished face,
the color of flesh, hooded
in drenched black fur,
fetal, a mere six inches,
hands clamped with tallow.
I sluiced him up
with the garden rake,
and held him there
dripping through the tines.
From the east,
across the vast Pisgah,
the sun glistered from its cave
on Mount Mitchell.
Light prilled upon us.

The Coal Miner's Wife: A Letter

(after Ezra Pound's adaptation, from the Chinese, of Li Po's "The River-Merchant's Wife: A Letter")

Southern women have alabaster skin.
　　—LI PO

We were from the same town, Cowen,
along the Gauley, Webster
County—church, twice of Sunday,
Wednesday evening prayer meeting.

I swore to every whit of it.
Hair chopped in bangs across my brow,
I played in moonflowers
and bleeding hearts.

Subterranean even as a boy,
feats were nothing to you.
You crawled the culvert
pipe to save Blind Ruby's kitten,

one eye blue, the other mahogany.
Its affliction was deafness—
plague of the white feline.
It could not hear thunder.

Rain unfolded from the sky,
another flood coming on,
my father, as yours, deep in the pit,
my mother silent as plums.

What happened to that kitten?
Blind Ruby's trailer ripped loose
when the branch leapt its bank.
Sycamores bent over the eddies.

You whispered in my ear. Before that sentence,
there had been nobody.
At fourteen, we married.
As foretold, you went to the mines,

left Mondays the scullery saltbox
with your pail, and drove off for wages
underground in Fayette County.
Never you pressed me. Never I shied,

nor from the rag to scrub the black—
what you could not reach when,
after years in the pit, hunched,
you could only so far lift your arms.

Five months, now, I have not seen you,
save your smudged letters—
your endearments in smoke:
My Darling. Coyotes weep

from the cliffs above the Gauley's white water.
I plant every genus of dahlia,
emerald moss at the doorsill.
It is September 3rd, the anniversary

of my father's death in Elkins Coalfield—
seven years now.
Billings' meadow has not been threshed.
The buckeyes refuse to fall.

Queen Anne's lace prospers.
Butterfly bushes grand as pipe organs.
Yesterday, on Agnes Ridge,
I saw an albino woolly worm—

auguring snow or manna, one.
Let me know you're coming.
I will trek out to meet you
as far as Camden-on-Gauley.

Light at the Seam

This is the afterlife,
threshold of oblivion:
a blacktop crest
on Pine Mountain,
Bell County, Kentucky,
US Route 119 burning
north through the heart
of coal until it plays out,
frozen, in DuBois, PA.
Out of gauzy lavender fog,
the wakened sun
swoons in white robes:
Jesus, flanked by Moses
and Elijah, transfigured,
*up into a high mountain
apart.* Deep within,
miners suspire,
shake light at the seam.

CPSIA information can be obtained
at www.ICGtesting.com
Printed in the USA
LVHW011713300322
714725LV00011B/1337